HELP DURING GRIEF

Hope for the Hurting

J. Mark and Kathy Ammerman

WinePress Publishing  *Mukilteo, WA 98275*

Help During Grief
Copyright © 1996 J. Mark and Kathy Ammerman

Published by WinePress Publishing
PO Box 1406
Mukilteo, WA 98275

Cover by **DENHAM**DESIGN, Everett, WA

Printed in Canada on recycled paper.

ISBN 1-883893-44-5

In loving memory and honor of
Sherry Lee VanEenwyk Ammerman
and
Jerry J. Serefine
who continue to influence our lives.

i

CONTENTS

Acknowledgments

With loving thanks and appreciation to
Charles Silk
Barb Conley
Sharon Chernoff
Faith Community Church
who saw us through the grief and recovery cycles
of our lives.

INTRODUCTION

Help During Grief explores the agony and despair of having lost a loved one. It is an experience that can only be understood by having been there. It throws you into a cycle that you do not want, did not ask for, and will hate to experience, but it is a cycle that must be completed. Understanding the steps can benefit and expedite the process.

You will go through the grief cycle sooner or later in your life. You will also know others who will experience the cycle and by knowing the following information you will be better prepared to assist them through the ugliest, most hurtful time of their lives.

The grief cycle and recovery time has been written about and identified in many ways. We believe the complete cycle can more or less be identified in four basic steps: 1) Shock, 2) Agony of Grief, 3) Negative response, 4) Positive response. Obviously, this can be dissected into many parts, but the general understanding can be grasped in this concept.

The old school of thought is that the cycle takes about one year to complete. The more realistic theory is that it takes about three years or so. The length will be determined according to each person's makeup, relationship with or without God, and the support he receives or fails to receive from family and friends.

This book attempts to explain and examine some of the emotional sensations you may experience during and after the death of a loved one. It scrutinizes the agony and despair of the survivor, primarily the spouse of the deceased. We have attempted to identify the feelings of losing a loved one, the shock that one is thrust into, the momentous agony of grief that follows, the negative responses, and finally, the hopeful positive responses.

This is not so much information on recovery, as information on hopelessness and anguish. This information describes the first realm that is encountered, identifying with the death of a loved one and attempting to masticate this knowledge in order to accept it as reality. This hurtful experience sets you, the survivor, apart from others. The survivor now has a new understanding, an understanding that is no longer naive about the most final stage in this world, the stage of death and its aftermath.

If you are in grief, you will surely recognize yourself and see that others have been there, each in his own way. If you know someone in deep grief, you will better understand what hopelessness means and see there is nothing you can do to "make it better." If you have not experienced grief, be thankful. If you have, you may find comfort in this.

"I Want To Die"

What is beauty without love
What is the family hearth
without the one who gave birth
What is victory
without the one to share joy
What is in continuing
without the one to encourage
What is the husband
without the wife
Without my friend
What is life?

Mark

Chapter 1

MARK'S STORY

Kathy entered my life one night over the telephone. She was contemplating suicide and was reaching out for one last strand of hope. Her husband, Jerry, had died recently of a heart attack and she was in total despair. She wanted to know if I would come and talk with her. I did, and a few months later while out to dinner together I realized this woman was a total surprise. I had a stir of hope, a excited but cautious premonition that this particular woman might end my eight lonely years of dreary limbo.

My father, Chaplain Jim Ammerman, sagacious counselor, informed me later that I had failed to act professionally because I had allowed emotions to enter into the relationship with a counselee. However, since this transference did lead to marriage, he blessed me anyway.

In a different life I (Mark) was married to my first wife, Sherry. She was the quintessential pastor's wife. Our family consisted of two daughters, Rebekah and Elisabeth. We enjoyed our faith, hope, and love, collectively growing in God. We were fundamental, Spirit-filled Christians. I, pastoring the church and Sherry, principal of our Christian school.

We had an unusual outreach ministry — bikers, primarily the Hell's Angels on the East Coast. It was with this intent that we were on my bike the night Sherry was killed. We had ridden into the city on my motorcycle to continue the ministry to bikers and dancers. It had been a successful night. Sherry had been able to pray with a dancer and we both were happy and excited for what had taken place.

It started raining on the way home. I remember thinking the rain would damage Sherry's new suede coat. The last few miles were foggy and wet so we were riding slowly, thus able to talk about the happenings of that night. As I stopped for the last traffic light, Sherry said, "I'm glad you're driving this big machine." Then we started down the straight stretch of the dark country road toward home when the bike hydroplaned. I knew we were going down. I remember thinking, *I'm sliding a long way*, and put my hands down to stop myself.

I sat stupefied on the side of the road and called for Sherry, but there was no answer. I thought, *this is going to upset her.* I called again, but to no avail. I began to search for her. The bike was stuck in the ditch so I couldn't use the headlight. There were no streetlights and it was too dark to really see anything clearly. I shouted continuously for her, feeling in the road for where she might be lying. I ran up and down attempting to find her, afraid a truck would pass by and run over her. Just over an hour later a truck did come by and I flagged it down. We found Sherry beyond where the bike had landed. No wonder I hadn't been able to find her. Having previously been a Kansas City police officer, I had seen plenty of fatalities and seeing the way Sherry was folded in half I knew she was dead. I unfolded her, watched her head roll with a broken neck like a rag doll. The truck driver went for help.

I started talking to her like I always did, only she would not respond. I lay in the ditch holding her, claiming all the faith verses I could recall, shouting commands to come back, pleading with God, "With both our faiths, it's possible; with the agreement of two or more where God is in the midst... Sherry help, tell Him you want to come back. Our ministry is not finished. It has always been us together. We have to be together."

The policeman wouldn't tell me she was dead. He was going to let the doctor do that. I was just sitting in the police car detached from reality. The ambulance crew was working on her in the ditch, but I knew. They took her to the hospital in the ambulance and I followed in the police car.

It felt like everybody in the emergency room was looking at me. The doctor wanted me to come into his office. I could see Sherry's feet under the sheet. He had done all he could and he said he was sorry. He asked if I wanted some time with her.

I remember saying, "Sherry don't do this to us. What am I going to tell our daughters? They're home sleeping on the front porch. You are full of life, everybody says so. This cannot be. You believe the Scriptures about having the right to live three-score and ten years. What about the stories we've heard others tell of hovering over their beds in hospitals and then coming back into their bodies. Sherry, together we can believe. God will answer that. It's His Word. Make it happen honey, now. Tell Him it is not your time. Sherry, I love you, you know that. I did not mean for this to happen. Sherry, please. I love you, you know it. Sherry, please!

"I don't want to stop touching you. If I stop touching you, they will make me leave. Honey, I love you. They have taken all your clothes off, except your panties. That would embarrass you, someone seeing your breasts. The damn ambulance crew— they didn't need to cut your blouse open. At least your panties are on and they aren't the Harley set I gave you for a joke. That really would be an embarrassment for you.

"You don't belong under this sheet. Holding her feet with her partially webbed toes I said, "At least you won't have cold feet anymore; you always complained about being cold. If I turn around they will make me leave. I feel them looking at me. Can you come back if I leave? Or does that make it final?

"An elder and a deacon are here with me and you are still dead. I don't want to leave, but it is time."

I hoped the lights from the patrol car would not wake the girls. They were going to need all the sleep they could get. They were going to need all the strength they had and more." God please stop this." I begged.

The first step in the grief cycle is the sudden shock of being informed of the situation. The death of a loved one or any major trauma situation in your life can create shock. When shock comes, you will be saying "No" to the situation either to someone or to yourself. *This cannot be* will shout in your head. You will want everything to stop and return to what it was, return to normal. You won't be playing a part, you will actually expect this to happen. When someone else tells you, "It's okay, you'll get through this," it won't be okay, and you won't want to hear their comments. Their comments won't register because you will want this to stop so much. You will want this impossibility to go away and life to be like it is supposed to be. The loved one, the security is supposed to be there.

I had to notify Sherry's family. I couldn't let them find it out on the morning news or secondhand. *How do I tell her father, who trusts God and loves his daughter?* At 7 a.m. people started arriving. I knew the cars were going to wake the girls, and sure enough, Rebekah and Elisabeth both were standing there looking at me. They knew something was wrong, terribly wrong. Rebekah asked, "Who died? Grand-dad? Uncle Bill? No? Who then?"

"Girls, we need to go upstairs and talk." Oh, the innocence in their faces. The fear in their precious faces.

Sitting on Libby's bed would never be the same again. They didn't want to hear it. "Girls, what I'm going to tell you is going to hurt so you need to be prepared. Your mother and I were coming home on the motorcycle last night and we had a wreck."

Rebekah asked, "Where is Mom?"

"Girls, there were four of us and now there are only three."

God help me, the piercing scream couldn't be coming from Libby. The deep groan, the hollow expulsion. I can still hear Rebekah shouting "No." It was horrible. I couldn't stop them from hurting. The screaming would not stop. The crying and the questions were coming too fast to answer. "Rebekah and Elisabeth, I am sorry," was all I could say. Neither would let me hold them.

I could hear the questions, but the answers were so empty. "I didn't get to tell Mommy goodbye last night." "Did she say anything?" "Where is she?" "Can we see her?" God, how I wished I had died.

We had a private viewing, just my daughters and I. How ominous and sinister, yet antiseptically clean the viewing room was. We stood there with the doors closed, just the three of us. I had an arm around each of them. We didn't know what to do or say. The girls approached the casket and looked at their mother.

You do not know what to say at these times. Your mind is attempting to compute this information and it is just not wired to do so. It is an impossibility, it's inconceivable, it just is not happening. "No" is the response to the shock.

Shock creates a latent period in your life. A thousand thoughts dart through your mind, yet your mind refuses to think or function properly. You can see, you can hear, you can listen and even make decisions, but not with clarity. Everything seems detached and indifferent. It is like groping for stability that is just out of your reach and unattainable, but you know it should be there.

Libby touched Sherry and wanted to know why she felt "hard." She pulled out a piece of cloth she had sewn. It said, "Thank-you for being a good mother," and she laid it across Sherry's arms.

How do you say a final good-bye to your wife, friend, lover, and soul-mate, the one you love? Walking out of the funeral home felt like such a violation of allegiance and faith. During the night I had an "encounter" with Sherry's voice instructing me to "be strong, courageous . . . " I woke to greet her and lost the conversation. I hugged the wall where she was speaking from, but could not bring her back. God, it hurt. I tried sharing the event with Libby, but she started crying and wanted to know why Sherry did not come and talk to her, since she had not been able to tell her mother good-bye. It hurt us both so bad, I did not bring it up again. I am well aware of the theological implications on whether the dead can or cannot communicate with the living. I am also well aware of the hell and groping torment of the night and the desire to converse with a loved one.

Viewing the body and deciding who else should, can only be answered by the closest loved ones. Walking into the room is shocking, but the experience of facing death is the first step toward handling grief. It's an oxymoron, you have to hurt first to begin healing. Needed realization of death comes with viewing the body and the close, loving good-byes need to be said. It is a feeling of ties and a breaking of them that must take place. It is a final picture that will be burned into your mind forever. Take the opportunity and take your time. It helps to have someone with you for support, but make sure you have time alone for personal, departing words. The event shreds your heart, but it is your heart's love that is communicating finality. Facing the problem is the first step toward healing. Of course, at this time the word healing is obscene. You don't want healing, you want your loved one back!

Agony of grief is the second step in the cycle. "Grieving is as natural as crying when you are hurt or sleeping when you are tired. It is nature's way of healing a broken heart."[1]

One of the wisest comments I have read came from Reverend Doug Manning's book, *Don't Take My Grief Away*. He used that title after he had heard a lady in torment and sorrow make the comment to a person who was attempting to make her stop grieving. That comment made Manning search his past for how many times he had tried to take the agony of grief away from people. He wondered how many times he had denied them the right to grieve. He wondered how many times he had attempted to fill the air with philosophical statements, to succumb to the idea that sympathy was somehow harmful. He wondered how many times he had taken away grief by sheer neglect, robbed a person of grief in his efforts to avoid it. Each person needs his own personal time and way to grieve and get through the agony. The steps must be gone through or they will return later to haunt and destroy the person either emotionally or physically. Do not let others rob you of what is normal and healthy grieving and the anguish that goes with it. The agony of grief is necessary. It is not your enemy, you must continue through the process.

"What ifs" don't work. You cannot change anything in the past, but you can improve the present and prepare for the future. Often this improvement comes by stating the thoughts and feelings you are experiencing now. Declaring and conveying your present feelings of hurt, anger, outrage, fear, confusion, or whatever is healthy and needed. It is cathartic and therapeutic. It cleanses the soul and with each episode loosens the chains of despair.

When your mind is on overload and ready to short-circuit, tell people what you want, and don't concern yourself with their opinions or feelings. You and your immediate family are going to be the only ones that this death is going to change completely. The others will leave and their lives will return to normal—yours will not.

Some people will look at the situation and feel pity for you, or love for you; but they look at you in a situation they do not understand and are not comfortable with. Experiencing a death, divorce, suicide, or incarceration makes you different. Even if others are not looking at you, you feel they are; and most of all this is a reminder of the magnification of the loss. You feel vulnerable, exposed, and defenseless.

I did not know anyone could go to a funeral parlor and shop for caskets. There was row after row of caskets. It was like shopping in Wal-Mart, but for dead people. When I entered the room and saw all that was available, I realized I was going to put my wife into the ground. This was final. This was real. My knees were undependable and I looked for a place to sit down. The funeral director and my father were saying something to me, but all I knew was I wanted out of there.

I chose one of the cheapest caskets and a flat stone in the colors Sherry would like. Later I wished I had chosen an upright stone. She deserved better. I had part of her favorite Scripture verse inscribed on it, "A Tree of Righteousness" and later wished I had her Christian bookstore name and verse inscribed on it, "Flower of the Field." I state this for a reason. There are many things to do and decide and no matter what your decisions are, you will wish later some had been decided differently. You did the best you could at the time. Remember that, you did the best you could.

I gave my wife's funeral. It was the way she had said she would want it. The church was full with many believers as well as nonbelievers. "Rejoicing and salvation" were the themes for the day, just like we were taught and what she would have desired. Only it was hollow. A funeral should memorialize the loved one and comfort the family. At the time, hope is slipping away, and the loved one departing. Anguish is incapacitating. My heart ached while my mind wondered. I held her feet, that was the last I touched her. She trusted me. She hated being on that bike, but got on it anyway. She was determined to be part of everything I was involved in. It happened on a Tuesday night. She should have been home preparing the Christian school curriculum for the following day. She was not at school that next day; she had never before missed school.

Three days since the death and I didn't want to see anybody. Christ rose in three days; it could happen. Sherry had that kind of faith. She prayed for a nephew to come back from crib death. She believed. The hospital could call. What a testimony that would be. Sherry could do that.

It was nice. The church was full. Pastors always want full churches. It was crazy — singing praise songs at a funeral, but that is what she said she wanted. All those glorious proclamations seemed so empty, so mocking.

There were plenty of bikers with their women there. *Maybe,* I thought, *they will get saved today and make it worthwhile.* But then I thought, *nothing was worth this. I wouldn't trade her for the salvation of all the bikers in the world.*

Chapter 2

KATHY'S STORY

I (Kathy) was just finishing my shower late in the afternoon when the phone rang. "Mrs. Serefine, this is the YMCA calling. Don't panic, but your husband is having trouble breathing." I asked if he had lost consciousness. They replied that he had and told me to please go to the hospital.

The ride to the hospital was grueling. I got behind an old man who would not go faster than 30 mph on a country road, and there was not opportunity to pass him. When I got into the city limits, and was a block from the hospital, I entered a school zone and was then stuck behind some law-abiding citizen who went the legal limit of just 15 mph. My emotions ran back and forth between *calm down, it's probably nothing*, to the worst possible scenarios.

Upon arriving at the emergency room, I was met by a nurse who had grown up with Jerry. I was to discover later that not only was she an incredible nurse, but pretty good actress too. Mary Jo told me that she had seen them bring Jerry in, but had no idea how he was. She directed me to a private waiting room. A room, I found out later, that they always put people in who are going to be told of a death of their loved one. She told me that it would probably be a long wait until we heard anything, and she asked if there were a couple of friends I could call that might come and sit with me until we did hear something. I, innocently, gave her the names of two close friends and she called them. She also thought we ought to call Jerry's mom since it would be a long wait and she knew his mother would want to see him when the time came. She waited with me until my friends arrived and then she casually said she would go and see if she could get some information on his condition. I found out later that this is when she informed the doctor that I could now be told the truth about my husband.

A female doctor entered the room, followed by Mary Jo. The first thing I noticed was that Mary Jo was crying, but at the same moment the doctor started saying these horrible words — "Mrs. Serefine, I did all I could for your husband; I'm sorry but your husband is dead." I immediately jumped up and screamed, "You're lying, you are lying to me. *Stop* lying!!! Jerry would not do that to me. Stop it!!!" I told them that if he was dead then they would have to prove it. I would have to see it with my own eyes because Jerry would never leave me, never! Although they hadn't "cleaned him up," they took me right to him and the moment I saw him all doubts left. He was dead.

Jerry was not a conceited man, but was very proud and would never have let anyone see him looking so ghastly. I just stared at him in shocked wonder and suddenly my entire future passed before my eyes. I saw our children graduating from school, getting married, accomplishing, enjoying life, and now he would miss it all! The only thing I could say, over and over, was "I'm so sorry baby." As I finally turned to leave him, my mind was numb. I had never been this alone before. I felt like my whole body had suffered an electrical shock. It was actually buzzing. It was like a Twilight Zone episode where everything looks normal, but is just slightly crooked.

I immediately thought of our kids, Andrew ten and Rachel fourteen. How would I tell them? What would I say? They knew I had been called to the hospital, but that was it. How to do it? Just do it: short, to the point.

"At 6:10 tonight your dad died of a heart attack while exercising at the YMCA."

The screaming was more than I could bear. I had no comfort to give, yet what else did I have for them? Their protection from the world was gone. *I was all they had!* And that scared me so much.

Friends took over throughout the ordeal of the funeral. We had a private viewing before the wake, and it was pitiful to see the kids physically yearn for their father; and me, so helpless to give them what they could never have again—their dad. The word inadequate took on a new meaning for me.

After the funeral, after spreading the ashes, and after a couple of weeks, life was returning to normal for everyone—but us. For us, normal was a continuing nightmare. I was a woman whose life centered around her husband and a teacher who was now on summer vacation. For me, it was beyond being a nightmare. There are no words to fully describe it.

The grief process is built into us, which is reason enough to suggest that it is the only way for us to deal with loss, emotional turmoil, and pain. If we abort that process or try to go through it quickly, we end up in an atmosphere of emotional dishonesty. There will remain a deep reservoir of anger and resentment.

Dr. Robert Hemfelt identifies the stages through which every grieving person passes as: "one—shock and denial, two—anger, three—depression, four—bargaining and magic, and five—resolution and acceptance."[2]

I (Mark) feel grief can be understood better if viewed as four basic steps that are seen within a circle. The steps are shock, agony, negative response and positive response. I put them within a circle because they are so interchangeable. You may go in a clockwise direction for a few hours or days, and then suddenly you are going counterclockwise. You experience each stage several times and in no particular order. It is confusing and upsetting.

Under the normal steps of grief, you do not need a therapist to progress through the stages. If you become stuck in a step along the way, that is when you need guidance from either a close friend or a counselor. You need to back up through the stages and repeat them as needed until the blockage breaks loose and grief proceeds in its required course.

The first experience with death is always the hardest because you have nothing to base the experience on. At forty, none of my friends had been through this so I (Kathy) had no one's experience to base mine on. But then again, I was too numb to know what questions to ask anyway.

I did take comfort in the certain knowledge that because we had been so special to each other that he definitely would be back. Maybe no one else had ever had their spouse come back, but I *knew* it would be different for us. Jerry would not do this to me. Upon the second anniversary of his death I told myself he would definitely come to me now. After all, I had now grieved to the point where hysteria was not an issue any longer. I could handle seeing him briefly and be able to let go. I went to the place I had spread his ashes, a bluff overlooking Keuka Lake, and waited. I was absolutely astounded and devastated when he did not appear. Thank God no one was around because I became hysterical over this, and being alone really let it out— complete with screaming, kicking my car and literally jumping up and down. Did it make me feel better? Not at all, only deflated.

The need to liberate the hidden, seething anger that is there is a must. You must acknowledge it, deal with it, and release it. Anger is a natural, healthy emotion for dealing with pain and loss. You must come to an awareness of your anger. Only by getting in touch with it can you put it behind you. We are not creating anger, we are flushing it out.

"There is good evidence that deeply held and repressed anger can suppress the immune system of the body."[3] It is healthy to identify and be honest with your emotional anger. You must turn it into an accomplice to health. Identify it and examine it. Express it and get to know it for what it is. For example I (Kathy) was painting trim on a rental house Jerry and I owned. I had been apprehensive about buying the house to begin with. Then Jerry died and within two months of his death our tenants moved out. So there I was having to get it ready to be rented and I was angry. I was so angry in fact, that after painting for an hour and getting paint all over the window, I picked up the three-quarters full bucket and flung it at the house screaming in frustration. All it did for me was embarrass me. Mark talked with me about it and made me see that of course I was angry and it had to be expressed in some way. When I realized other people do things of this nature and that it is normal, not just wasteful energy that I really "should" control, I felt so much better. In doing this you will take control over anger instead of it having control over you. Failure to deal adequately with anger will result in expressions of depression, addictions, or other self-destructive mechanisms. Depression is anger turned inward.

I had never been prone to depression. I always saw the bright side of living. That part of me was now gone. Depression became a constant, maybe the only thing I felt I could definitely count on. I did not know you could physically feel pain from a broken heart, but you can. I did not know I could cry as many tears as I did and still have more to shed. Depression became my ugly little friend.

Jerry never realized the depth of my love for him because I did not know its depth. I did not know love went that deep, yet I had never taken him for granted in our marriage. I always felt so thankful for our relationship. The bottom of the barrel for me was when I knew I would do anything to get him back—no sacrifice was too great to make. I did not care who I had to kill or let be killed if it meant he could come back. It was a depraved thought, one I am not proud to admit even to myself. I cared about nothing and no one. I knew I should be "better" for my children, but the fact is I wasn't, and I didn't care.

Everything was backwards. When going through a loss, thought patterns are often out of focus, they are not lined up with clear thinking. Your world suddenly becomes turned upside down and nothing appears real. Your understanding is off, and this will last for a long period of time. To try and make yourself think right or differently is an impossibility at this point. Things I would have assumed would bother a widowed person didn't bother me—like still working out at the place where Jerry died. Things, however, that did bother me were things like grocery shopping—everything I bought from toilet paper to ice cream was tied to Jerry. My biggest question was why are we allowed to love so much only to lose so badly! People cared, but my grief made me untouchable to receive comfort. The only one who could truly comfort me was irrevocably gone. There was nothing I could do to fix that. Frustration was constantly there.

I do not think I ever thought of Jerry as many times a day while he was living as I did now. Preoccupied thoughts of your loved one will become obsessional with you. Small details will be thought about for hours, or reminders of the past will lock you into that time zone as if you are there again. You will want to straighten out your thinking, but your thoughts have been uprooted and they leave you thinking crooked.

The lack of clear thinking is generally seen shortly after the death and you sense the presence of your loved one with you. Different stimuli will trigger these thoughts such as a smell, a certain place where the two of you had a loving experience or a good time. Then again, sometimes for no special reason at all, it will occur.

A few weeks after the death I surfaced from grief just long enough to inject myself with a generous helping of guilt over being burdensome to people. It seemed I needed so much and had absolutely nothing to reciprocate with. This was the case for almost eighteen months. This was not helped by the fact that my mother passed away eleven months after Jerry. She had been sick with emphysema for six years, but she had been such a comfort to me, having been widowed herself, that when she died a tremendous source of strength and understanding for me was also irrevocably taken away. I was very aware of how needy I was, but was helpless to rectify it. Many people feel ashamed of normal grief behaviors such as being depressed or self-centered when it is really self-preservation and required for healing.

When you think no one understands and you are all alone, you are right. You are not nuts. Only you can know the feelings and thoughts you are encountering. However, I felt by the second anniversary of the death that I was getting better about it until I received a long letter from my sister, a counselor, telling me that "everyone" thought that it was about time I got on with things; after all, it had been two years. She really could not understand my selfishness nor, according to her, could anyone else. This letter undid a lot of my progress. Death seems to remove your barriers from hurt and you have to rebuild. That letter destroyed a good portion of my newly built, fragile barriers, and down to the bottom I went again. Others, who I now know would be labeled co-dependents also tried to "help" me.

A time of defeat is an opportunity for a codependent to find an opening into your life, and start controlling. He will give advice and you are too weak to oppose or care. He will start "fixing" your life for you and you will respond to him. You can barely continue to live. The codependent may mesh his life with yours, as if the two of you have become one. Thus you become codependent or literally dependent on him. It appears he is helping, but in reality he is repressing you and thwarting your progress.

One person who assumed this position in my life threw up her hands in disgust at me one day and in an exasperated tone of voice announced that she was only trying to "put this family back together again." It was a real wake-up call for me because no one could do this, and more importantly, no one had asked her to do it. She had seemed so understanding at first, but it was almost like she then used all I had confided in her to convince herself that she knew what was best for me. She viewed my vulnerability as a complete inability on my part to lead my life. She was trying to take over what was left of my life. It scared me. My sister, Sharon, on the other hand was totally understanding and would constantly encourage any sign of strength in me.

As soon as you are strong enough to start living again, you will need to identify any codependency problems in your life. So, beware of the advice giver. He could be a codependent who is lacking fulfillment in his own life and is searching for self-importance, self-acceptance, and control in your life. Codependency can be an addiction to people, behaviors, or things. To the codependent, control or lack of it, is central to his life. A healthy person who offers help will applaud your progress and encourage you to keep on striving.

Chapter 3

FRIENDS

Close friends seemed to desert me (Kathy) within months of Jerry's death! I still had a couple of friends, but not many. The person who is truly a friend will be in evidence at the time of the grief cycle and recovery. He will give of his time, patience, understanding, and will suffer right along with you. He will believe in you, and will hope for you to recover. He will endure the long time needed for recovery after all others have gone about their lives and have forgotten about you. Most of all, his love will never quit.

The true friend I (Mark) had during my ordeal was Charlie Silk, a man who was there for me even when I did not know I needed help. He listened to my anger, hurt, and frustration. He cried with me and laughed with me. He shared good memories about my wife with me. He was there long hours, and yet was able to give me my desired time alone. He kept everything entrusted to him in confidence. He was my friend.

A friend who will be the most helpful to you will be the good listener who is nonjudgmental, accepting, able to hear the bad as well as the good, and not be afraid of anger. The person who is not your friend is the listener who is not helpful. Doug Manning in *Don't Take My Grief Away My Grief*, says:

> The unhelpful listener will say that talking doesn't do any good, counsels not to be weak (i.e., express too much pain or sadness), urges you to think of others who are worse off, sees the female's expression of anger as unladylike, not maternal, frightening, or sexually unattractive. Will see the male's expression of sadness, longing, or despair as being unmanly, a waste of time, an indication of impending collapse, and urges you to focus on tomorrow and forget the past.[4]

Now is a needed time to evaluate the criterion of friendship.

"The fact is, all relationships change—for better or for worse—over time. That's why it's crucial to scrutinize your friendships periodically—to determine which are strong, which don't work anymore, and which can be categorized differently."[5]

Discomfort while in the presence of a friend or after having been with one, can indicate the lack of acceptance, affirmation, or affection. Realizing that you are now a different person than before your tragedy and that you now have different needs and certainly different understanding, may make you re-evaluate the friendship you once had, and may make you realize that it is no longer a healthy one.

With uncertainty and perplexity, even with some guilt, you may need to decide to be friends from a distance.

The next time you feel uneasy about being with an old friend or relative, ask yourself: Does he or she accept me for who I am now? Does he/she give me the acceptance, affirmation and affection that I truly need? If not, be thankful for the good times you had together and make the decision to move on to healthy relationships in which you can both give and receive the needed unconditional love.

It helps to know that friends are often at a loss for words when you need them, not because they do not care—they do, but because they are so overcome with befuddlement that they do not know what to say or do. In reminiscing about Jerry's death, his friend, Geneva, New York's renowned psychologist Joseph DeMeis, stated:

> Thinking back on Jerry's death, and my first reaction after hearing the news, I think of how it couldn't have happened. I think about how Jerry died and how none of us could help him or stop it from happening. The unfairness of the death was prominent in my mind. How could a nice guy who followed the rules die so quickly

without a hint that it was going to happen?

Some of the reasons friends don't know what to
say is that they feel helpless or embarrassed. They
feel "sorry" and it sounds so inadequate. Here are
five suggestions for helping a friend in grief from
Susan McClelland's, *If There's Anything I Can Do*:

> **One** - If you're going to speak your
> sorry-ness, keep your statement
> simple and then keep going. The goal
> is to get to the point where you can
> handle "I'm sorry" in such a way that
> the friend you've spoken to doesn't
> have to talk about IT.

> **Two** - Show how you feel by putting
> your arms around your troubled
> friend. This is a powerful antidote to
> misery.

> **Three** - Beware of gossip. Personal
> misfortunes, unlike illness or injury,
> bring about a whole web of unveri-
> fied rumor, half-truths, and innuen-
> does.

> **Four** - Be prepared for failure. Go
> ahead and assume that your friend
> will respond brusquely. It can happen.

> **Five** - And do be in touch, whatever
> the response to "I'm sorry." Days from

now, when too many friends drift
away, figuring the "worst is over,"
your reminders that you haven't forgotten can be a big, big help. The
"worst" can be a long, lonely road.[6]

The long, lonely road can be dissected with
helpful way-stations of encouragement that are
timely for the one hurting. A major way to help and
receive help is from a simple note of encouragement.
Jerry died in mid-June. At the end of August I
(Kathy) received a note from a woman he had
worked with. She apologized for waiting so long to
get in touch, and then went on to write a very
touching letter. Receiving that note at that time was
such a comfort to me. By then I thought that
everyone but me was doing well. It was just what I
needed at that point. The advantage of a note over a
phone call is that its brevity can convey real
sympathy over and over as it is read by the bereaved.

About a month after Jerry's death, I (Mark) wrote
Kathy a note that simply stated:

Dear Mrs. Serefine,

Knowing from experience that
words and good intentions help little,
I would still like to say we are pray-
ing for you and your children. I did
not know Jerry more than to say
"hello," but do know from observation
you were a close family and a good
example to the community.

If there is any way I can help from sharing what I experienced with the death of my wife and learning the grief cycle and recovery, to using our swimming pool or taking you on a hot-air balloon ride, please let me know. Don't feel odd in asking, I know an escape from the waves of shock and grief often are needed and we are just across the corner from you.

Mark, Rebekah, and Elisabeth

When Kathy was ready to talk, she gave me a call because she knew I was there.

A friend will offer help and will be flexible when needed. Take them up on their offer. If friends are willing, do not hesitate to give them a call. No matter what time it is. Do not hesitate to accept their willingness to help.

Mrs. Sandy Braverman, a woman we met through the writing of this book, recalls the salvation others were to her after her mother passed away, while at the same time her father was in the hospital. Friends offered to run needed errands, make purchases at the store, drop something off at the hospital, and many other deeds that helped to reduce the pressures of the day. When friends say they are there to help, let them. If they found it an inconvenience, they wouldn't offer and they receive encouragement by giving encouragement.

On the other hand, Kathy remembers: "If I had been told before the death that certain people were going to distance themselves from me, there is no way I would have believed it; nor would Jerry. I had no clues as to why they did it and it hurt so much. There is a mourning involved in that too. I not only had the death of my husband to mourn, but the loss of people whom I thought would lend me unconditional support. I felt so scared when this happened."

With a death comes the feeling of rejection anyway. Rejection that can tear at the very soul of you and your desire to live. No matter if you are an adult or child, the feeling of rejection leaves you feeling isolated and empty. With this feeling or understanding it is hard, if not impossible, to build a sound structure to live by and to give meaning to life.

People are created to have relationships — ones that give us identity, self-worth, security, acceptance, and most of all, love. The litmus test for having accepted the monster of rejection is, "Are you bitter?" Bitterness is an identifying characteristic of rejection. It blinds you, lies to you, and can destroy you.

Chapter 4

NEGATIVE RESPONSES

I (Kathy) know now the cruelest thing you can wish on someone is not that they will die, but that the one they love the most will. You want the pain to go away so badly. The negative responses will often occur in the following areas:

> **One** - Radical religious involvement. This generally causes you to seek and respond to "deep" religious involvement. A spiritual answer is sought, the "hidden" meaning of life and death are expounded upon. Not only is there a desire to be close to God, but there is the consuming desire to see God in

everything. During this experience, others generally turn away from you and consider you a "religious fanatic."

Two - Promiscuity. Different thoughts attempt to justify this, such as, "I played by the rules the first time and lost, so why not?" or, "I have lost my partner, so I will have sex with whomever I choose." There is a need for the personal touch, the caring relationship, the emotional fulfillment, the understanding that can only be met by closeness.

Three - Turning to drugs (legal or illegal) and alcohol. There is a need to numb the emotional feelings and to distance yourself from their destruction. Logic has no place here. There is just the prevailing longing to stop the thoughts and feelings that are crushing your soul mentally and emotionally.

I (Mark) got drunk one night. I did not normally drink, but just decided I didn't care. I wanted to stop hurting and stop thinking. The next day a faithful friend at church took me aside and told me that if I was going to get drunk, to please not do it on Saturday night, because I reeked on Sunday morning. I had assumed it was such a secret and in reality it was shouted from the housetops.

I got drunk because I just didn't care anymore. I got drunk at home. I was not about to let anybody see me. I could not tarnish my image. I was too strong for that. I even waited for my two daughters to go to bed and gave them time to get to sleep. After I got drunk, I would go to bed to sleep it off and wake up later sick. I would then roll out of bed onto the floor, crawl into the bathroom and vomit in the shower. I would sit on the floor of the shower until the hot water ran out and the cold water brought an inspired revelation...this is dumb!

We can get so righteous when we are dressed properly and it is daylight and the secrets of our heart are hidden, but this is the negative response part of grief.

Another area of negative responses can be the overwhelming desire to commit suicide. It is amazing the myriad of material that is written for "after the fact" help, instead of "during the event" crises. The "shameful" thoughts and intents are never discussed or honestly acknowledged. You may feel isolated because you don't know others who have experienced the same contemplations and private battles.

One morning at 5:00 a.m., I was sitting on my kitchen porch steps, in my undershorts, my heart broken, my head wanting the hurt to stop, and knowing the .38 cal. Smith & Wesson pistol I was holding would put a stop to it all. I did not fear eternity, the afterlife, or even contemplate what God thought about it. I did not care in the least. My only question was, *Who would take care of my daughters?*

I could not bear thinking of them hurting anymore than they already were. I needed to be around to help them. It was a hapless life and I wanted out. Suicide was not a question, I knew I could do that. I just didn't want my daughters to hurt anymore. My next illogical thought was *why not kill them too?* Only I knew I could not hurt them, so I just sat there dying inside.

When did I decide I hated God? All of my taught theology as a minister said do not blame God. Others counseled me not to, but I would reply, "I am not blaming God, leave me alone." Then one day, while alone in church, I stood up and shouted, "God, I hate you. I hate you. I hate you." And I meant it with all my being. Death in its rage had split my family pointlessly and vindictively. People asked me, "Oh, you didn't say that, did you?" But, yes, I did. God knew what I was thinking anyway, so why not be honest?

I (Kathy) used to go into my closet and bury my face in Jerry's clothes, just to smell him. One day I did and his smell had faded. The brief comfort I had gotten from this was gone. That was the day I got rid of his clothes. It seemed all around me there was betrayal—his death, perceived abandonment by friends, old comforts becoming cold comforts. I know this is when I entered the negative response stage of grief.

Grief will go into you deeper than you ever believed possible. There is a sense of emptiness that comes at this time. Nothing can fill it for there is no bottom to it, so there is nothing to build on. This emptiness causes a void that nobody can fill because the oneness you had with that person is gone. During this time the "ifs" come. What if — I had driven better, what if — we had not gone there, what if —

we had spent more time together. The "if" brings with it anger, bitterness, and blaming. You can blame yourself or you can blame the person. Why did you do that to me? Why did you leave me? Why did you pull that stunt? You blame the very person you love the most. You blame others who give advice, or others who are trying to help. You blame them because they do not know the situation or what you are feeling; so here comes blame with a capital B.

During this period your entire life and experiences are shrouded in misery, sorrow, and anguish. It is somewhat like living in a portable coffin. You are not dead, but don't know why not. You would just as soon be dead. Despair is the key word for the day, especially at night or during the quiet times. You literally pine away for the loved one.

With each new decision, you wonder what the "other" would think or say about it. With each common action you have performed a thousand times, you remember the loved one's involvement. The day-to-day travelings reveal past experiences of togetherness.

The emotional suffering caused by bereavement contaminates the entire soul — the mind — in the way you think and process data, the emotions — in that they are senseless and in chaos, the will — in that it refuses to function properly. You will for things to return to normal, but they don't.

This can also change your entire personality forever. There is a new knowledge that has been manifested and the innocence of the old cannot be restored. With this comes the revelation that trust is broken and innocence is tainted with an ugly reality. Only those who have experienced this despair can understand the heaviness and isolation of grief.

The worst part of the death and abandonment by friends is that your sense of trust is destroyed. This in turn destroys your self-confidence.

I (Kathy) would avoid people. In a store if I spotted a person I knew, I would try to slip by unnoticed rather than risk being snubbed or treated coolly. Still, today, when I enter a public place, I sometimes find myself scanning the area to see if I recognize people so I can go the other way. For so long I was sure no one liked me. The cruel realization was that those who turned away were really Jerry's friends, not mine, and I just never knew it. Jerry, the link for my relationship to these people was now gone, so the relationship naturally ended too. I can't fault these people any more, now that I understand this. However, at the time this knowledge made me question my judgment of everything. If I could be so wrong about people I thought I knew so well, what else was I wrong about? I did not have the courage to find out. At forty you cannot say to people, "Why don't you like me?" They either will not tell you or worse, they might, and I couldn't stand it either way.

Chapter 5

BOUNDARIES

Boundaries in our personal lives are needed in order to separate life-ministering thoughts from destructive thoughts and healthy friends from noxious people.

The person who sets boundaries and lives by them, knows who he is. He is confident, friendly and authoritative. He knows where he is and where he is going in life. Most of all, he has decided what he will accept or no longer accept in life. He is in control.

Kathy and I have a totally different set of rules and boundaries since experiencing the grief cycle and others' responses to us during it. Helped by understanding the importance and demands of our boundaries, we are "overcomers." We do not accept derogatory remarks from others. But even more important, we do not accept it in our thoughts or in our concept of living.

By setting clear boundaries in our own minds and then sharing them with others, we affirm and declare ourselves intellectually, emotionally, physically, and in relationships. This allows us to grow in confidence, and at the same time it wards off rejection or betrayal. It creates a fulfillment in our expectations.

Boundaries are not walls and are most effective when flexible, allowing for change and growth. With boundaries you can determine who gets close to you physically and psychologically, and who does not. It is essential to establish your boundaries for what you need emotionally during the grief cycle and recovery.

If you have not before, now is the time to choose to be active rather than passive, pro-active rather than re-active. Remember to stay flexible and adaptable, do not become rigid and unfeeling toward others. I (Kathy) asked a twice-widowed man I knew how to adjust and cope. He told me to accept every invitation I received, but to always drive myself to the event so I could leave if I started to feel uncomfortable. This was good advice and people who invited me were very understanding about it also. This allowed me to be flexible while trying to adapt to life without Jerry.

An indication that boundaries have been established is the elimination of the black-white statements of absolutes, phrases such as "always", "everybody", "must", "should." During your emotional down time others probably came to help you and gave you their advice. Now even though you are recovering, they still want to help. They are still telling you what you "should" do. The first step in freeing yourself from this is identifying it, and the second step is confronting the other person with it. Stay flexible and stay in charge.

The strength and emotional power you will feel by doing this is amazing. It not only puts you in charge, it frees you from the despondency of the past. You will have a new awareness that you are no longer the victim, but are becoming an overcomer, a survivor.

There are some excellent reasons to set boundaries and live by them. They are not restrictive, but liberating, empowering.

Being empowered has dual consequences. It is liberating as well as threatening. At this time in your life you want to set new boundaries to be empowered and to start ruling again. You want to be free and yet it is all a little intimidating.

A major key to success and overcoming is to keep healthy, challenging, life-ministering thoughts in your life and only allow safe people to get close to you. Safe people will listen to you and accept your opinions and feelings. They will be clear and honest with you, supportive and loyal. You will have a sense of gratification, accomplishment, and inner peace after being with them and discussing such thoughts.

The challenge is to choose this boundary on a daily basis. After three to four weeks, you will start to feel and think this way automatically. You will have a sense of overcoming, a sense of achievement, and satisfaction. You will actually start realizing you are in control again.

Another key to being an overcomer is to accept what is yours and reject what is not. Develop an awareness of your inner life, your expectations, and know the dynamics of both. You must know that you and you alone are given the authority and are responsible for your success. Nobody can make you "feel" anything without your consent. Nobody can crawl into your head.

Being able to understand the difference between healthy and toxic thoughts and people involves steps which one has to take to establish healthy boundaries and get rid of the hindering ones. For a healthy concept, you must first name it, know what you want, and identify it. Secondly, you must own it and experience it. You must make it a reality, if only for a moment and experience it. Thirdly, you must associate with it. Think of the benefits and feelings, and envision the difference it will make in your life.

I (Kathy) was such a good 1950s kind of obedient wife. I always deferred to my husband, so I had to accept the concept of being in charge. What I had to learn to want was independence and I had to identify ways to do that. I remember my first shaky step toward being in charge was writing checks to pay bills. Since previously I had written only one check a week for groceries, this was quite an experience.

You likewise need to clarify your vision of success and embrace it so that you will believe it while it comes to fruition. Do something continually to build a "super highway" of faith in your newly found knowledge.

The steps to eliminate the toxic thoughts are: first, put a name on it for what it is and identify the destructive element in it. Second, identify the consequences of owning it. Third, identify where it is coming from. And fourth, let go of it. Know it will not be allowed in your boundary anymore. There is no longer any room for it.

Look for good results which will be: you will know who you are; you will feel good about it; you will no longer let a bad situation control you.

Once you learn to think healthy thoughts they will serve you and you will be saved by them. This will set you free. With toxic thoughts you will be snared by them. This will oppress you and bring you into subjection of destructive elements and relationships. Having healthy boundaries is crucial for recovering and establishing directions in your life.

Controlling your thoughts is easier said than done. People are constantly coming to me (Mark) with problems in their thought lives. They want to know if I can handle a "bomb." I always say that I probably can. They then tell me their thoughts and I patiently wait and reply, "Where is the bomb?" This always surprises them and defuses the bomb at the same time.

In your grief cycle and recovery, as in your day-to-day life, you will not have any new "bomb" or thought that has not been thought before.

Someone once said, "Thoughts are like birds, you can't stop them from landing on your head, but you can stop them from building a nest there." A constructive way of bringing every thought into captivity is by admitting you have the destructive thoughts (and not being shocked that you do), and using them as a tool to succeed. As someone else once said, "The best way to get rid of an enemy is to make him into a friend."

Decide ahead of time that when the wrong thought comes you will use it to remind yourself of something good. For example, if you see someone who has made a hurtful remark, don't become angry. Instead, decide they will be a reminder to you to be thankful for all the good people in your life.

No matter what has happened, no matter what the outcome is, you have chosen to respond strongly and victoriously. Consequently, you are in control, not the other person, remark, or thought. They do not have to change, but you have changed. You have decided the results.

By having no boundaries, I (Kathy) found I lived with what I perceived as abandonment from many sides, uncertainty and fear. With all this in me, how was I now expected to heal? I had my cousin telling me six weeks after the death to stop crying so much or no one was going to want to be around me. Was I selfish, totally self-centered — you bet! The real question was — did I have a choice — the answer is NO! What the world saw as my being self-centered and selfish was in reality my spirit fighting to survive. I felt like I was falling down a well, alone.

When you have to force yourself to just get through minutes in the day, it is not possible to evaluate if you are being thoughtful of others. You don't care. You desperately need people, yet your feeling is that you want to be left alone. Healthy emotions are a must in order to continue and succeed in life.

Love, forgiveness, and life are what you are created to have. "Ninety percent of the people in hospitals are not ill due to an accident. They are there because their insides are eating them up."[7] The emotion that is destroying them is the emotion of guilt. "If only I had . . ., If only I did . . ., I should have . . ., If only I had not . . ., " and the list goes on forever. Suffering is a very easy trait to keep, it comes naturally, you do not have to work for it. But love and forgiveness are hard and must be continually worked for.

It takes courage to choose life, love, and forgiveness, to work at liberating yourself from guilt or suffering but it is possible.

The need to be emotionally healed is evident in not only how you feel at the moment, but in that we are emotionally led individuals. We would like to believe that we are intellectually led but psychology, the business world, and honest self-evaluation proves the "85/15 Formula" is true. "We make decisions based on 85 percent of our feelings and only 15 percent on the cold, hard facts. We may use the facts to help justify a decision we want to make, but we generally make our decisions for emotional reasons."[8]

With this understanding there comes a time that you must choose to become emotionally healed and complete. This is the healing process that develops on its own and the healing process is a decision that must be made. A decision that says, "I choose to be healed, to stop hurting, to live again in as much completeness as possible." It's a choice to control the emotional feelings in your life. An hour-by-hour, day-to-day choice — to be healed.

Chapter 6

TENSION UNITS

Before the death I (Kathy) was a great mom — a Brownie leader, Girl Scout leader, Cub Scout leader, softball coach. I gave great birthday parties. I always baked cookies. A lot of quality time was spent with the kids. We were a real throwback to the 1950s kind of family. I shut down when Jerry died. Mealtimes were a thing of the past. Bedtime was something the kids completely took care of for themselves. Seeing me as a strong woman was a thing of the past. Those articles and ads on warm family scenes used to reflect my life — college sweethearts, still in love after nineteen years, more in love with each passing year. We were a walking cliche. When I see these articles and ads now, I feel an emptiness. Before the death I never realized that emptiness is definitely a feeling.

We are created to be fulfilled and complete, as well as taught to think in complete accomplishments. Therefore, when we have incompleteness in our lives, there is tension that builds up in our mind's subconscious. This creates what Jack Canfield terms "T.U.s" or tension units.[9]

T.U.s are tension units we carry in our intellect and emotions. If we do not dispose of them properly, they will cause us emotional and even physical problems. We are only made to carry so much tension, and right now you are probably carrying an overload. To say nothing about grief and despair, there is also the lack of strength it causes and the inability to think with clarity. In addition there are also all the other considerations that are involved with day-to-day living. These are all T.U.s, tension units that are building up.

To start unloading the T.U.s you can do as suggested by Canfield: "do, delegate, or dump."[10]

For example, Look at an unfinished project, do it (finish it), delegate it (give it to someone else to do), or dump it (get rid of it). As quickly as you do this, you will feel free of a T.U. You will automatically feel somewhat better.

I (Mark) hired a cleaning lady during the years of being "single again," came home to a clean house and felt free, stronger, and more complete. I switched to perennials in the yard and now I was free next spring. Do anything that will help you feel complete. It strengthens you.

Do, delegate, or dump is a refreshing concept. It is a major way of removing stress. Most importantly for the sake of your subconscious, do not carry guilt when you rid yourself of these pressures.

As you are becoming free of T.U.s, remember that motion establishes emotion and it is your emotions that you are attempting to strengthen. If you can clap your hands at a party, or shout at a game, or wave your arms to someone with delight, then you have created emotions from your motions. They are also examples of being free of tension units. Next time you accomplish a release of a T.U.—clap your hands, or shout, or wave your arms—watch how your emotions are encouraged and strengthened.

It certainly sounds funny or even embarrassing at first, but as you have decided to become strong and remove tension from your life, you are celebrating with motion. If you have finally cleaned a room or accomplished some other task you were not able to perform before, walk around the room with your hands up in the air. With clenched fists shout, "I did it, I accomplished it, I overcame." As humorous as it sounds, it works. You are created to overcome, to be complete and tension free.

Take time and compliment yourself if you make it through a day or half a day without crying, cursing, or feeling depressed. Shout when you feel the least bit of success.

Attempt at least twice a day to sense the emotional freedom that helps condition your emotions. What you continually search for is what you ultimately find.

And what you ultimately should want to find is complete healing. It strengthens not only the body but the soul as well. Rest is needed during recovery and the proverb "Sleep is sweet to the working man" identifies not only the need for mental challenge, but for the physical as well.

Physical exercise enhances self-image as well as assists in relieving depression, stress and anxiety. With higher self-esteem, we are better equipped to cope with life's adversities, we are more resilient, more creative in our work, successful, ambitious, and have a fuller sense of life — emotionally, creatively, and spiritually. "Self-esteem is the reputation we acquire with ourselves."[11]

By having a regular exercise program for a minimum of twenty minutes a day, three or four days a week, positive mood swings increase in a short three weeks. This helps you fight off the destructive emotional feelings such as depression, anger and guilt. These emotions and self-esteem are linked together.

These strengthened positive moods can be used as a weapon that will help you combat the ugly feelings that can engulf you and bring you down. You will feel stronger both emotionally and physically.

Don't kid yourself though, exercise on a regular basis might be the last thing you think you can do, but please give it a try. It works. You may not want to do it, but give it a try.

Chapter 7

SLOW HEALING

When does grief become self-pity? After three years I (Kathy) still felt like I was dying on the inside. Did that mean I had crossed the line into total self-pity? Sometimes I thought how normal I looked to others. However, if they were to scratch my surface they would see that at times I was inwardly crying with sadness. You will feel like you are acting much of the time. The weird thing is that no one but you will know. You will appear to be absolutely normal.

The loss of a loved one can send you into deep despair and withdrawal with long periods of crying, insomnia, and suicidal feelings. Other indications of grieving will be displayed and should be considered "normal abnormalities."

Distorted and mythical thinking is often a by-product of this. There is often a denial of reality involving the loved one's memories. I have found

47

the best way to make a "saint" of someone is to have them die. There comes a feeling of abandonment and devastating results for those left living. As with any sudden death, there is the feeling of helplessness.

It does not take a mental problem to commit suicide. It merely is the decision to stop hurting. It is a reality, it can happen, and it should not be taken lightly or inadvisably if the topic is broached. Also shock, anger, or denunciation should not be the response to the topic, but instead love, concern and encouragement.

Some of the uncomplicated mourning signs are sadness, anger, guilt, and self-reproach, anxiety, loneliness, fatigue, helplessness, shock, yearning for the lost person, and numbness. Beyond the emotional feelings there are the cognitive thoughts of disbelief like, *I will wake up and this will be over.* There will be confusion, difficulty concentrating, preoccupation and obsession with thoughts about the deceased, thoughts such as sense of presence; that the person is somehow still here in hallucinations, both visual and auditory. For example you may think you hear the loved one say your name or smell the presence and believe the loved one is really there.

Mark and I married eight months after Jerry's death. People who had begun to distance themselves from me now felt they had a bona fide reason — I had abandoned my dead husband in a shockingly short time. "How could I do this," they asked? "After all, what would you do if he suddenly came back?" Intelligent people actually asked me that question.

You will not believe some of the things people will say to you. The most incredible thing about these questions is that they will be ones you dealt with long ago in your mind. The person assumes you never even considered the question. It is almost like they feel it is their duty to ask you the question to bring you to your senses. In addition to the fact you lost your loved one, they think you've lost your common sense too. After all, in their eyes you aren't behaving rationally — but remember, that is their opinion.

A helpful revelation concerning the remarks you will hear after a death is that there will always be those for you as well as against you, and the largest segment of people in between who do not care at all about you. As you digest this knowledge and find healthy, encouraging and supportive relationships, you will benefit and recover more readily.

In the caring relationship, the person will always be ready to talk, encourage, and most of all listen. Much of the time as the survivor of a death you need to verbalize the experience repeatedly, thus attempting to relive the last minutes of the loved one's life and continue the affiliation. No matter how many times they have heard it, the wise and loving friend will listen, agree, and give the understanding feedback needed. Search and find this person. He is a life preserver for you.

As in all of life there are those who will come against you with their opinions. They have absolutely no concept of what you are experiencing, but will give their opinions anyway. Though some will be decidedly vicious, most will mean well. An excellent example is while at my (Mark) uncle's funeral another uncle overheard my aunt (the widow) say she was going to sell the house and move to an isolated location. He responded by saying— "You don't want to do that, you will never find another husband there." This is the type of opinion that should not be voiced. You will have to be on guard so as not to be hurt by them.

There are three different groups of people you may encounter. Those who do not know what to say, so they say nothing. Those who do not know your situation so they obviously don't comment. How the rest of the world does not know your loved one has died and you are devastated is beyond your comprehension. Finally there are those who are afraid of their own mortality or that of their spouse. They try to avoid you, usually subconsciously, because you are too vivid a symbol of what can happen in real life.

There was obviously so much people did not understand about my (Kathy's) situation. Jerry was a wonderful man, my best friend who thought I was the funniest person he ever knew. A friend commented to me that she had seen us just before Jerry died and had thought to herself how evident it was that we loved each other. If I was home for the day, he would call me from his office at least three times just to chat. When he died, the void that was immediately there was bottomless.

I had been through the death of my spouse and I offered to talk to Kathy if she ever felt the need. On the lowest night of her life, two months after the death, a friend insisted that she call me. I went by and offered the understanding of one who had walked in her shoes. I did not give her any false hope, but instead understood her desperation. I told her it would not get better for a very long time, but she *could* make it—not *would* make it, just that she *could* if she chose. We continued to meet to talk and within a short time we grew close.

I saw the real her and so did she, for maybe the first time. You will find the real you too, and there will be things about the real you that you will not want to believe.

The real you will be made of weak desperation. Some people will probably tell you how strong you are but you will know it is not strength. It is merely a person who is not dead, but not alive either. You will feel as if you can barely move and you will be amazed that it is viewed as strength.

I (Kathy) had no strength to put on any false identity. I was confused, sad beyond reason, and totally without hope. I was afraid of everything, yet fearful of nothing, a walking oxymoron. Death no longer scared me, yet going to the store did — that is what I mean by feeling confused.

Mark understood this, and my impatience that would sometimes cause explosive behavior. He helped me realize that it was natural to be angry and that I did not have to be ashamed.

My reason for marrying so soon after my husband's death was that I was lonely and here was a man who understood this. He wanted to make a life with me. He knew after grieving himself for so many years what I was going through and would continue to go through. He was prepared. He did not feel threatened by the memory of Jerry. He even went so far as to give me permission to pretend that he was Jerry when we made love, if that gave me comfort. His understanding did not make my hurt any less. Nothing could. The reason Mark could do this was that he had been where I was. This definitely gives a person an astounding amount of understanding.

On our honeymoon we both realized that there would always be four of us because Jerry would always be a part of Kathy as Sherry would always be a part of me. This was all right because they had helped make us the people we were. Do not feel that eventually you will have to forget your loved one. You will not. The loved one will, as time goes on, assume a place in your life that will fit. Do not let others convince you otherwise. Because of our understanding of this truth, Jerry and Sherry remain very much alive to our children.

My (Kathy's) mother and my children were the biggest supporters of my remarriage. Mother had been widowed herself and knew the despair. My children realized that my heart was broken and felt that if there was someone who could bring me happiness and comfort, I should do it. As my daughter Rachel said, it was not like Jerry and I had divorced; he had died and I was forced to live. I had no choice in that.

When the one you love dies, your ability to love does not die. The need to be needed still exists. For a while it gets buried in grief but it does resurface, not because you want it to, but because it is a part of you. You have to face a lot of needs you do not want to have. That is something people who have never lost anyone don't understand. These are needs that demand attention. In the best of all worlds these needs should stay hidden, but then again in the best of all worlds you would not be widowed.

I (Kathy) also found that with my remarriage there was not instant relief from grief. The bad times were still intensely bad. I simply had someone to hold my hand through it. He could not take it away. Brace yourself for that. No one, no drug, no drink will take away your pain, at least for any length of time. The hurt is far too painful because it travels from your heart to your head and back again, and it replays itself countless times.

The hurt is all inside and is all-consuming for a very long time. Misery loves company and that is the role Mark played. He helped me by letting me know I was not crazy to feel as I did and still do today. In almost every other happening in our lives we are told to work through it and put it behind us. This is impossible to do with the death of a loved one. There is no truer saying than "Where there is life there is hope," and that is what makes accepting the death of your loved one so hard. He is no longer alive, so there is no hope, only despair. You will never get another chance to be with that person and that is the hardest part to accept.

One of the things that will make you crazy is the little things that catch your attention for a brief moment, but open up a floodgate of hurt. Things like the way one person in a couple reaches out and touches the other, catching the way someone tosses his head to the side, or walks just the way your loved one did. Maybe it will be the way a stranger wears his hair or you will hear a new song and know how much your loved one would have liked it.

Things like hearing new songs, seeing new movies, watching a restaurant you used to go to together go out of business, are all painful markers of a bygone time for you.

Sleep problems are also prevalent among widowed people. I (Kathy) had very life-like dreams for about eighteen months after the death. These often will only make your grief worse because the loved one is so alive again, and then you wake up and realize that it was all in your mind. It will make you angry and physically weak.

In order to start reversing the emotional effects of the death, you need to admit what has transpired. You will not want to or feel like it, but you must. The sensation that accompanies this is like having to shake hands with a fiend that has conquered. Doing so is a paramount decision on your part. This will start putting you in control instead of being controlled by outside influences such as emotional ups and downs, others' comments, and random thoughts, or even the temperature of the day.

Making the conscious decision to accept what has happened gives "conscious purpose." Thus you take the responsibility for formulating and creating the desired outcome in your life, that of recovery.

With recovery comes the need of a strengthened self-esteem. Once the formidable task of acceptance has been accomplished, then resolution comes. With resolution you have now come to terms with your past and are no longer enslaved by it. Your present life is now workable and the future just might be better, at least there are glimpses of hope.

Chapter 8

MARK'S POSITIVE RESPONSE

I know exactly when I (Mark) crossed over into the "Positive Response" area that contained flickers of hope and the temptation to want to live again. I also know I had concluded the cycle at three years and two months after my wife's death. I know the date that I realized I had the ability to make the choice to live again. I understood I was whole enough to start or continue looking forward to the future instead of remaining in the past. Remember, so many decisions are choices, but you have to wait until you have the strength to make them.

At that time I realized the grief cycle was completed and that I could continue to live because my wife would always be part of me. I had been afraid to close the final gap of the cycle fearing I would have to put my wife away and she would not be part of me, nor as close if I did. I was afraid to take the final step because I did not want to abandon memories of her either in my mind or heart.

When I realized my wife was still part of me, as well as this grief cycle, I could start to live again without the guilt of abandonment on my part. With my wife part of me, I could take my memories of her and her love, and continue my life.

I had my wife's name and her favorite flower tattooed on my chest. One day an individual saw it and made the comment, "You'll have to live with that the rest of your life." Well, that is why I put it there. Because whether I married again or not, Sherry would always be a part of me, a very large and strengthening part of me.

Sherry and I became "one" in our souls. We were soul mates in the way we thought, believed and lived by faith. We were soul mates in our very existence. To know me is to know Sherry. I knew then, a second spouse would have to understand we would never have the same type of love as the first relationship did. We could possibly have the best second marriage that we could develop, but we would never have the oneness of the first marriage or its understanding, its innocence.

I could maybe have the best second marriage ever, but that spouse would have to understand that she would have to take a different place. I wondered if I would ever find a woman who could accept that. Every time this woman would see me without a shirt on and observe the tattoo, she would also know the name was down inside my heart, because Sherry is forever part of me.

When I realized my wife was part of my makeup, I realized I could continue without guilt, without grief. I could live again, but now, more knowledgeable and with more understanding.

There are moments of hope. During this positive response time you will try new adventures that will give you hope and encouragement. It is during this passage the finality of the cycle begins to be seen in the distance. During this time your mind is still bombarded with doubts and hopes, accelerated peaks and valleys.

Everybody told me that with the death of my wife it would take about a year to recover. At the end of a year nothing was different. At the end of two years still nothing was different. The mind will go through this cycle in a week, a month, even a day. One hour you are encouraged and the next you are devastated. Overall, the cycle will speed through your head like a little clock in your brain, but down in your heart there is a larger clock turning much much slower. The small clock in your head turns fast and frequently. It is the surface level of thinking. It will take you through all the steps — shock, agony of grief, negative response, positive response, in an hour, a day, a week, a situation, an event, a memory. It occurs with rapidity and lunacy. There is no guarding against it nor preparing for it. It just happens.

The large clock is the clock of the heart, and is in the depth of your being. It turns much more slowly and methodically. It turns and transforms you as you journey through the grief cycle recovery process. There will be true emotional progress only as this clock turns and you experience one whole cycle and its events, and are then ready to progress into the next. The damage, the cleansing and the healing take place as your heart is restored and strengthened, as your thinking returns to normal. While your head will travel through all the feelings in a day, down inside you are moving at an inchworm's pace.

You need to be honest about the cycle, both with yourself and with others. You need to know where you are and how to cope. The ignorance of not knowing the cycle will cause problems if you are trying to help in a counseling situation. Without knowing the cycle you might assume your advice will be helpful, but it might not be if you don't know where the person is in his/her mind or heart. Comments like, "It's okay" are made, but it is not okay, and to hear such a thing is an insult to the person in grief.

Two years and two months after the death, I realized I was in a grief cycle. It took me a year to journey through shock and another year to accomplish the heavy agony of grief. I was two months into the negative response and I was becoming very angry. I was becoming very bitter and spiteful.

I hated anybody who had ever dared to speak against my wife. If anything was said or even hinted at that was not respectful or reverencing of Sherry, I was ready to strike. This ate at me. I either had to conquer this or resign from the ministry.

By sharing these truths with others and developing a grief cycle teaching it helped me to slowly start responding positively. I could see that I had taken a year to go through shock, a year through grief, and only two months into negative response, I knew I would not make it through a year of this stage. It would destroy me and my ministry.

If you want to be able to help yourself or other people you need to know where you or they are emotionally and spiritually. You need to know the stages you will go through. You need discernment and understanding.

God did not come to kill, steal, or destroy. So do not let somebody tell you God took your loved one, or God did that to get your attention, or God knows best and that is why He did this. That is ignorant religious advice and is not of God.

Chapter 9

A CHILD'S RESPONSE

Our children's responses to the news and aftermath of the death will forever echo in our hearts. My (Mark's) daughters walking into the room the morning after and standing there in their pajamas knowing something was terribly wrong but afraid to ask, will be forever burned in my memory.

Ascending the stairs to their bedroom to tell them of the tragedy and then informing them was the hardest thing I have ever done or ever will do in my life. After that experience, everything in life seems so diminutive and unimportant. Other problems seem foolish and insignificant. Too much was taken away to be threatened with anything else. The Malthusian belief of overpopulation, global warming, another Great Depression, the bomb, or even Armageddon. So what? Please do not waste my time. The breaking of our children's hearts breaks ours even more.

As I watch my children and my wife's, I realize that adolescents have their hands full just trying to establish who they are and finding their own identities in life. It is hard to separate from their families physically, financially, and emotionally. In doing so, they need to feel their families, and certainly their parents, are there for them when needed. This supplies the basic need of security. If a parent has been taken from them in death, the needed security and love is ripped from them and even more uncertainty of their identity is heaped upon them.

For people to understand the grieving process, and especially the timing, it is essential to understanding where the survivors are emotionally. The year of intense grief and pain is sometimes extended for the adolescent. Karen Gravelle says in *Teenagers Face to Face with Bereavement,* "It's usually about a year before you can talk about it. Because before you can tell people about it, you have to accept it. And it takes a while for that."[12]

> As reality focuses, the initial denial, shock, and depression give way, exposing a range of agonizing and often conflicting feelings. Added to the usual intense and confusing emotions typical of adolescence, the pain, anger, and guilt of bereavement present grieving teenagers with a lot to handle.[13]

The concept could be compared to dumping a truckload of weight onto a mini car and expecting it to pull through. It is just not made to handle that much, nor is the child created to handle such devastation.

Guilt and regret are seen and identified with comments like, "I didn't get to say goodbye", or "I should have done . . . ."

The worse thing for my (Kathy's) daughter Rachel was knowing that the last thing she ever said to her father was "I hate you" when she talked to him on the phone an hour before he died. They'd had some minor argument that at age fourteen she had blown out of proportion. It continues to depress and haunt her even though as she grows older she comes to understand that things like this happen, and unfortunately you get no second chances when they do.

Having "stupid" thoughts and suicidal feelings as well, are all part of natural feelings. It is important to recognize and accept them as being all right to examine. These feelings are not something to be shamed with or told not to experience, or to be told to think differently. The surviving teens are doing the best they can, and if they are alive — that says a lot for them.

The death of a parent ". . . strikes a blow to a child's developing sense of trust and self-esteem, causing feelings of powerlessness and shame."[14]

Often with the sense of shame due to the loss, comes the feeling of being unworthy and unlovable. The child feels mortified and humiliated. The child will often exaggerate his inadequacies by going to extremes in the negative response area of the cycle. What is the difference in you secretly responding in an ugly manner, and they responding openly? The core problem here is not rebellion, but hurt disguised as shame and manifested in shameful acts. They are crying out for help and understanding—for wholeness again coupled with security and trust.

For children to feel shame or embarrassment over the death is so unfair, but is so very often the case. The embarrassment is due to the fact that you lost. Whenever destruction has been successful in your life, that is a defeat and defeat is an embarrassment. You are made to be successful. You expect to be successful. Part of their security is ripped away and they feel vulnerable and helpless.

The first Sunday back to church, after the funeral, I remember Elisabeth standing outside the front door of the church telling me, "I don't want to go in." At that time I did not understand my daughter's thinking pattern, but knew she needed emotional love and encouragement. She was embarrassed to face others.

In regard to embarrassment, I once heard a speaker say that some families feel successful if they can raise their children to graduate from high school without the daughter getting pregnant or the son being arrested. Then they feel they have succeeded. Such ugly fear of embarrassment and shallowness of love is seen in that comment.

Embarrassment is not devastation. You can live with it, it will pass. Relationships are more important than disappointments. The needed understanding and acceptance are virtues the friend should have for the person in need. Love is a needed balm that will help in the healing at this time. Confidence and trust are treasured attributes that are also needed. They help build lasting confidence and security between the loved ones.

Claudia Jewett identifies the need for positive interaction with both the internal comments and physical contacts. She equates the child's soul to a bucket and says:

> When a child loses or changes care-takers (parents), the bucket is "sloshed" and some of these good feelings about self and others are spilled. If the child has strong feelings of guilt and shame, he develops "leaks" in his bucket. Even if positive energy is available, the child's good feelings about himself and others are slowly drained out. The child may discount his need for positive energy or his ability to get it; he may shrug off positive strokes. The resulting depletion makes the child needy, demanding, and reluctant or unable to give back much to anyone."[15]

Many times parents, or those in authority, are directly responsible for emptying the buckets of the children. Adults need to constantly be on guard against focusing upon negative exchanges with the children. Negative interaction depletes so many of the good feelings the children need, especially during the time of recovery.

Children's self-identity is based on their parental acceptance. Their basic needs are met through communicated love and acceptance.

With the death of a loved one, the dual state of love with emptiness is created. The innate desire to love and be loved by the deceased is there. But at the same time, the emptiness of not being able to express the love to that person is overwhelming. The frustration is maddening. Nothing is concrete or absolute. The love cannot be expressed, while the emptiness sucks the life from you and you become nothing. Love makes you. Without love, you are nothing.

Someone asked if we don't feel we have spiritual responsibilities at this time. The answer is that during grief all your responsibilities are starkly evident to you, but the ability to fulfill most of them is crushed.

Chapter 10

MARK'S HURTFUL TRUTHS

While speaking to a church group in Dallas, a lady who had lost her husband in a car accident ninety days previously was introduced to me because her relatives were getting tired of her depression and crying. They knew of my situation and brought her to me so I could give her counsel. They were telling her, "Look, you have to go on with your life, it's been ninety days."

Her relatives wanted her delivered from grief so they could continue life as usual. I said, "You are still in shock, the worst is yet to come." Everyone looked at me like I was saying something dirty. I knew the grief and negative response was going to come before the positive response.

She asked me if it was going to get better or worse. I told her it was going to get worse before it got better. I told her it was going to be the closest thing to hell that she would ever have to experience. I told her it would then get better.

It was just by the grace of God that I wasn't dragged out into the parking lot and stoned. Everyone left me standing there because they did not want to hear such things, much less have me tell her that. Their idea was to create an instant miracle to heal her. Healing would come, but it would follow a path and it would be slow.

A year later she called me and told me what helped her through the experiences of the past year was that I told her hell was coming and she would understand when it arrived. She knew that she was not losing her mind when she got into those negative responses, and that she was not the only one in the world who had been there, or could understand.

Many people think that way. They believe they are going to lose their minds. They just want the hurt and grief to stop. That is where they are. That is reality to them. It is not a matter of saying "Keep a stiff upper lip, stand up and stop it."

We need to understand where people are and their ability or inability to respond. We need to be equipped to give proper advice, not well-meaning ignorant mandates.

Looking back, I (Mark) cannot believe some of the advice I was given by well-meaning people. Ninety days after the death of my wife, people expected me to start living again in a normal fashion, to be dating, looking for another marriage partner.

To me, this was about the most stupid advice I had ever heard. These were "spiritual" people too, my mentors, counselors and advisors—people who claimed they were hearing God. They were not.

I was still in shock, and the agony of grief was coming. Hell was coming. I was still numb, not believing what had happened, believing it might still go away; it might still just be a bad test or dream that might somehow end. Many people lead minimal lives, self-absorbed and insensitive, while others are drowning in hurt all around them. It is so hard to tell.

In daily conversations, comments and remarks from well-meaning people may be taken wrong. You can become over-sensitized and hear criticism where none is intended.

Ignorant comments are not only directed to the survivor, but can be expanded to others in peripheral relationships. Kris Rimlinger, a friend of the family, identifies such a comment:

> I was in labor the night Sherry was killed and gave birth at 12:23 the next morning. I was young and needed encouragement. What I received from another woman was the question,"Do you think there is a reason why your child was born the same night Sherry died?" What in the world is a comment like that supposed to mean, and how am I supposed to interpret it? It haunted me for a few years.

To be a friend to someone in the grief cycle, you must not ignore the fact that a death has occurred in the life of that person. Here are four fundamental guidelines for helping:

One: Do not withdraw from the survivor.

Two: Do not compare, evaluate, or judge.

Three: Do not expect sympathy for yourself.

Four: Do not patronize the survivor.[16]

At the risk of redundancy, I cannot emphasize enough the ignorance of well-meaning friends, relatives, and counselors who violate steps one and two. They withdraw from the survivor and make that person feel even more abandoned in life, and then turn right around and evaluate the person's life in total ignorance of experience. As someone once said, "We see things not as they are, but as we are."

The day I was burying my wife, I was in the yard hanging a swing in the tree with my two daughters, attempting to impede thoughts about the coming event. A totally self-absorbed individual drove up and proceeded to tell us how miserable he was over the death (he hardly knew my wife). I could just as easily have hung him as hung the swing. It wasn't his place to expect my comfort and yet he did.

People I (Kathy) worked with knew about my loss and I felt like I was under a microscope. Now it seemed everything I did was open to discussion and question. Prior to the death, I had been dieting; I needed to lose weight. After the death I did not have to diet, but I still lost weight.

People saw the weight loss as a reaction to the death, and my boss actually called me into his office and demanded to know why I was still losing weight. He also demanded to know answers to questions that were none of his business—like why I felt I had to return to work, why I had stopped going to counseling, and how I had the nerve to be seeing someone so soon after Jerry's death. He wondered if I knew everyone was talking about me. He told me he was just concerned for me, but I felt he was actually angry about it because he had known Jerry and his "rules" made it wrong for me to do this. I did not have the fortitude to stand up to him. This was in September.

The following June I was transferred to another building but had to endure another meeting with him. This was just one month after my mother's death. He told me that I had failed to be a team player that year, that I had spent too much time alone, not enough time in the staff lounge, and this made others uncomfortable. I was still in so much grief not only over Jerry, but also due to the death of my mother that I could not bring myself to do anything but cry.

What people do not appreciate is that for the first year or so after the death you are trying to do the best you can and you are painfully aware it is not as good as it was before the death. But the fact is, it is the best you have to give. Upon reflection I know now I made others too uncomfortable. You will find this also. When you find yourself confused as to why people are distant it is probably for that one simple reason. You have had an experience that others are afraid of having, and having to watch your pain is too distasteful. They don't want you to go away mad. They just want you to go away.

I found that people who give the most advice are often the least qualified to do so. They have not experienced a loss. If they had, they would know there are no pat answers.

Chapter 11

RIDE THE BULL

While preparing to ride a Brahma bull for the first time in a rodeo, I had the distinct impression that this is what life should be like — breaking out of a mundane existence and trying something totally beyond my control. Friends and spectators were quick to cheer me on, but they were definitely observers. When the cowboys were strapping me onto the bull, the sights, sounds, and smells were all confirmation that something new was about to happen.

The impending excitement was reinforced when I was strapped to the bull and told to put my tailbone on the bull's backbone without putting much weight on it. When I did, I watched the bull's muscles expand in all directions at once. While my amazement was also expanding, the bull collapsed in the pen. I was pulled head-long down into the chute with my boots still caught in the wooden barriers overhead. I remember thinking, *I'm hugging a bull, upside down.*

The cowboys were shouting down to me to "spur him." I up-righted myself as much as I could, while still being strapped on, and asked if that is what I should really do. They replied with a resounding "Yes, spur the bull," as they fled from the top of their safe perches. So, I spurred the bull.

I only thought I understood and was prepared for the ride which I instantly received as the bull roared up on his hind legs and attempted to vault over the chute wall.

I was amazed at how my mind could tabulate so much information at one time. I was trying to hold on and at the same time let go. I could hear the crowd cheering, the cowboys yelling something. I felt the pressure on my legs caught between the boards, knowing that I could be crushed. I was still thinking, *a black and white bull, I can do it.*

After calming the beast down, for he indeed had miraculously grown before my very eyes, I could hear the cowboys off in a distance instructing me about something. What I could hear most vividly, however, was the blood pumping in my head as the adrenaline screamed throughout my body. As I focused on reality, I saw a huge red nose looking at me and a clown telling me to listen to them. A cowboy was saying, "Nod your head, and we'll open the gate."

I did not want to nod my head. I knew what was going to happen if I did. But you only go around once! I nodded, the gate opened, we exited, and that bull went anywhere he wanted to go. All I remember is excruciating jarring and snapping and hearing hoof beats. Oh yes, you can hear hoof beats while you are falling off a bull. They sound like shovels digging into the ground, right beside your head.

I do not remember much of the ride or the fall. It was probably best summed up in the question a young boy from our church asked his mother, "Why did Pastor Ammerman go "Oof?" The ride was six seconds and I dislocated my wrist.

As I stood muddleheaded in the ring, the announcer was asking me how the ride was. The clown was yelling at me to watch out for the bull, the crowd was cheering, and I was looking at my hat on the ground and thinking, *my new cowboy hat is dirty*. I picked it up as the clown reached me and guided me out of the bull's way. I shouted to the announcer, "It was great," and left the arena to the applause of the crowd.

That is what I have found life to be like. Most people will be only spectators at best, never desiring nor understanding the thrill of the challenge. Some will even ridicule and jeer.

Others will be content to help and stay on the sidelines. This is fine as everyone is needed to make society complete.

But wholeness comes with challenge. It requires us to expand our horizons, to shake off the limitations that have been placed on us due to circumstance or catastrophe. Living life is taking the challenge to be whole in our spirit, soul, and body. To be overcomers, courageous, and healed is a choice. You can do it. Ride the bull.

KATHY'S EPILOGUE

It is now five and one-half years later for me. Things have gotten better, but it has been a very gradual evolution. Why is it that dramatic changes in our lives often occur unnoticed by us until after the fact? I remember exactly when I stopped crying for Jerry on a daily basis. It was three years and five months after his death, and I felt very guilty that the tears finally stopped. However, I don't remember exactly when I stopped thinking of him daily, or when I started to be able to think of our life together with warm thoughts instead of wrenching ones.

Recently, I watched a scene unfold that was like watching my former life. I was at the gym working out and a woman I knew was also there. Her husband appeared in the doorway, looked all around the room, spotted her and went over to talk to her. He wasn't dressed to work out; he'd just arrived but came to see her first. They talked for a couple of minutes and then he left to go change. This was the exact scenario Jerry and I used to follow. Watching that couple immediately brought Jerry to mind, but thinking of him brought about a different feeling from hurt. The kind of feeling I now experience is bittersweet. I'm able to smile now when things like that happen because of the good memories that scenes like the one at the gym bring to mind.

I have also trained myself to stop wishing for what can never be. Yes, you can train yourself to do this. You simply repeat over and over, "stop wishing for things that can never be." Eventually after you do this enough, the message sinks in.

I am finally at peace with the unalterable fact that Jerry can only be alive in my past, not in my current life. I don't feel any longer that it is a betrayal on my part to feel this way. I have faced the reality of the situation. This is probably the biggest change that came about gradually, my ability to accept the reality of things. This has carried over to other areas of my life as well.

My father-in-law, while visiting last summer, ministered at our church. I asked him to pray for me that the past would assume its rightful place in my life. At that point I still hurt so much sometimes, and I wanted to stop hurting—dare I say wanted to feel better? Finally the other night I realized that this prayer has been answered.

Rachel is going to graduate from college this spring. I wanted to give her something very special to mark the occasion. She doesn't have many keepsakes from her father, so I took Jerry's and my wedding rings and my two diamonds and had them melted down and made into a necklace. There was enough gold left so I thought I might, in the future, have one made for me too. When I brought the necklace home though, and tried it on to see how it looked, I felt I was truly wearing Rachel's necklace. It didn't feel right to be wearing it. The thought that passed through my mind automatically was "This jewelry is from my past, that is where it belongs, not in my present." I realized in that instant that I had made the transition and the past was finally where it belonged.

How did that make me feel? Very strange. I cried a little, but they were tears of relief that the past was finally in its rightful place. I was at last at peace with a reality that had been so overpowering and frightening just a few years before. I finally realize that the truth of the matter is that putting things in the past really means you put only the pain there. Jerry is still with me, but not obsessively or painfully anymore. He is in death what he was to me in life, a soothing, easygoing presence.

My cousin used to ask me if I would have become involved with Jerry if I'd known what I know now. She always asked me if it was worth the pain I had to go through. I hated that question, probably because half the time I wasn't sure what the real answer would be if I were to be completely truthful. Now, however, I do know the answer. The answer is yes. It was worth it. I am a better person because of Jerry Serefine having been such a significant part of my life and because of what the pain of his death taught me. I have memories that I will cherish and remember warmly for the rest of my life. They say that everything you experience has the ability to transform you if you let it. And I can say with certainty that the experience I had with Jerry, and that I continue to have today due to his death, has done just that for me.

MARK'S EPILOGUE

"It is well with my soul."

As the years have passed with all their added experiences, maturation has added wholeness and holiness to my life.

I have judged opinions, those I have sought out with validation of temporal and eternal truths, as well as unsolicited declarations that have only birthed wind.

King Solomon stated in Ecclesiastes 12:13, "Fear God, and keep his commandments; for this is the whole duty of man."

I know that "He who has begun a good work in me shall complete it."

Revelation 3:20-21 states, "Behold, I stand at the door, and knock; if any man hear my voice, and open the door, I will come in to him, and will sup with him, and he with me. To him that overcometh will I grant to sit with me in my throne, even as I also overcame, and am set down with my Father in his throne."

I have supped with death. I now sup daily with Life and that Life is eternal. He is the Lord Jesus Christ.

By His grace I have overcome and one day I *will* sit down with my Father who is in Heaven.

BIBLIOGRAPHY

Branden, Nathaniel. *How to Raise Your Self-Esteem*. New York: Bantam, 1990.

Canfield, Jack. "How to Build High Self-Esteem,": Nightingale, 1993 (Cassette).

Cowles, Phoebe. *McCalls*, "Friends for Life," April 1993.

Gee, Bobbie. *Winning the Image Game*. Berkeley, Page Mill 1991.

Gravelle, Karen. <u>*Teenagers Face to Face with Bereavement*</u>. Englewood Cliffs: Silver Burdett, 1989.

Jewett, Claudia L. *Helping Children Cope with Separation and Loss*. Harvard: Harvard Common, 1982.

Manning, Doug. *Don't Take My Grief Away*. New York: Harper/Row, 1984.

McClelland, Susan. *If There's Anything I Can Do*. Gainesville: Triad, 1990.

Straudacher, Carol. *Beyond Grief*. Oakland, New Harbinger, 1987.

ENDNOTES

1. Doug Manning. *Don't take My Grief Away*. (New York: Harper/Row, 1984), 60.

2. Ibid., 214.

3. Ibid., 223.

4. Ibid., 63.

5. Phoebe Cowles. "Friends For Life", *McCalls*, April 1993: 94.

6. Susan McClelland. *If There's Anything I Can Do*. (Gainesville: Triad, 1990), 141.

7. Ibid., 32.

8. Bobbie Gee. *Winning the Image Game*. Berkeley: Page Mill, 1991), 85.

9. Jack Canfield. "How To Build High Self-Esteem": Nightingale, 1993. Cassette.

10. Ibid.

11. Nathaniel Branden. *How to Raise Your Self-Esteem*. (New York: Bantam, 1990), 28.

12. Karen Gravelle. *Teenagers Face to Face with Bereavement*. (Englewood Cliffs: Silver Burdett, 1989), 3.

13. Ibid., 47.

14. Claudia L. Jewett. *Helping Children Cope with Seperation and Loss*. (Harvard: Harvard Common, 1982), 106.

15. Ibid., 110.

16. Carol Straudacher. *Beyond Grief*. (Oakland: New Harbinger, 1987), 224.

To order additional copies of

Help During Grief

please send $9.95 plus $2.50 for
shipping and handling to:

Genesis Bookstore
70 Seneca Street
Geneva, New York 14456

For quantity discounts please call
1-800-213-6162

The truths of this book can also be
purchased on tape.

For more personal and direct care, please call our
Help During Grief Hotline at

1-900-884-LOSS (5677)

Hours: 7:00 P.M. - Midnight EST.